# my first

# KNOCK-KNOCK JOKES

## Lots of Laugh-Out-Loud Jokes for Silly Kids

### Jimmy Niro

sourcebooks
wonderland

Published by Sourcebooks Wonderland, and imprint of Sourcebooks Kids.
P.O. Box 4410, Naperville, Illinois 60567-4410
(630) 961-3900
sourcebookskids.com

This product conforms to all applicable CPSC and CPSIA standards.
Source of Production: Versa Press, East Peoria, Illinois, USA
Date of Production: October 2020
Run Number: 5019496

Printed and bound in the United States of America.
VP 10 9 8 7 6 5 4 3 2 1

# TABLE OF CONTENTS

# NAME NONSENSE

Knock, knock.

Who's there?

Will.

Will who?

Will you let me in already?

LOL!

Knock, knock.

Who's there?

Alex.

Alex who?

Alex-plain later!

---

Knock, knock.

Who's there?

Jo.

Jo who?

Jo King! Get it?

Knock, knock.

Who's there?

Nicholas.

Nicholas who?

A Nicholas worth five pennies.

Knock, knock.

Who's there?

Gwen.

Gwen who?

Gwen can you come play outside?

Knock, knock.

Who's there?

Oscar.

Oscar who?

Oscar silly question, get a silly answer!

---

Knock, knock.

Who's there?

Conrad.

Conrad who?

Conrad-ulations! That was a good joke!

Knock, knock.

Who's there?

Ivor.

Ivor who?

Ivor you let me in or I'll climb through the window.

---

Knock, knock.

Who's there?

Abbot.

Abbot who?

Abbot you don't know who this is!

Knock, knock.

Who's there?

Theodore.

Theodore who?

Theodore was closed, so I knocked.

Hi!

Knock, knock.

Who's there?

Duncan.

Duncan, who?

Duncan basketballs is something I love to do!

Will you remember me in a minute?

Yes.

Will you remember me in a week?

Yes.

Knock, knock.

Who's there?

You didn't remember me!

Knock, knock.

Who's there?

Iona.

Iona who?

Iona new toy. Do you want to see it?

Knock, knock.

Who's there?

Iva.

Iva who?

Iva sore hand from all this knocking!

Knock, knock.

Who's there?

Alec.

Alec who?

Alec-tricity.
Shocking,
right?

Knock, knock.

Who's there?

Nobel.

Nobel who?

There's Nobel... that's why I had to knock!

Knock, knock.

Who's there?

Cher.

Cher who?

Cher would be nice to see you!

Knock, knock.

Who's there?

Hal.

Hal who?

Hal will you know if you don't let me in?

Knock, knock.

Who's there?

Déjà.

Déjà who?

Knock, knock.

Knock, knock.

Who's there?

Major.

Major who?

Major day with this joke, I bet!

Knock, knock.

Who's there?

Pharaoh.

Pharaoh
who?

Pharaoh enough!

Knock, knock.

Who's there?

Harry.

Harry who?

Harry up, it's cold out here!

Knock, knock.

Who's there?

Luke.

Luke who?

Luke through the peephole to find out.

---

Knock, knock.

Who's there?

Claire.

Claire who?

Claire the way, I'm coming through!

Knock, knock.

Who's there?

Police.

Police who?

Police, may I come in?

---

Knock, knock.

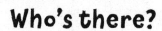

Who's there?

Doris.

Doris who?

Doris locked. Open up!

Knock, knock.

Who's there?

Benjamin.

Benjamin who?

Benjamin to my favorite song!

Knock, knock.

Who's there?

Haden.

Haden who?

Haden seek is my favorite game!

20

Knock, knock.

Who's there?

Alex.

Alex who?

Hey, Alex the questions around here!

---

Knock, knock.

Who's there?

Isabell.

Isabell who?

Is a bell working?

Knock, knock.

Who's there?

I am.

I am who?

You don't know who you are?

---

Knock, knock.

Who's there?

Otto.

Otto who?

Otto know what's taking you so long!

Knock, knock.

Who's there?

Dwayne.

Dwayne who?

Dwayne the bathtub. It's overflowing!

Knock, knock.

Who's there?

Ben.

Ben who?

Ben knocking for
ten minutes!

Knock, knock.

Who's there?

Howard.

Howard who?

Howard I know?

- - - - - - - - - - - - - - - - - - - - - - - - - - - -

Knock, knock.

Who's there?

Nana.

Nana who?

Nana your business.

Knock, knock.

Who's there?

Mikey.

Mikey who?

 Mikey doesn't fit in the hole!

---

Knock, knock.

Who's there?

Frank.

Frank who?

 Frank you for being my friend!

Knock, knock.

Who's there?

Amish.

Amish who?

Really? You don't look like a shoe!

Knock, knock.

Who's there?

A herd.

A herd who?

A herd you were home, so I came over!

Knock, knock.

Who's there?

Whale.

Whale who?

Whale, whale, whale, what do we have here?

Knock, knock.

Who's there?

Cows go.

Cows go who?

No silly, a cow goes *moooooooooo!*

- - - - - - - - - - - - - - - - - - - - - -

Knock, knock.

Who's there?

Kanga.

Kanga who?

Actually, it's kangaroo!

Knock, knock.

Who's there?

otter.

Otter who?

Let's get otter here, we're running late!

Knock, knock.

Who's there?

Rough.

Rough who?

Rough, rough!
I'm a dog!

(PRO TIP: Make the
punchline sound like
a dog bark!)

Knock, knock.

Who's there?

Dragon.

Dragon who?

These jokes are dragon on and on.

- - - - - - - - - - - - - - - - - - - -

Knock, knock.

Who's there?

Gorilla.

Gorilla who?

Gorilla me a hot dog, will you?

Knock, knock.

Who's there?

Aardvark.

Aardvark who?

Aardvark a hundred miles for you.

- - - - - - - - - - - - - - - -

Knock, knock.

Who's there?

Gopher.

Gopher who?

Gopher help! I'm stuck!

Knock, knock.

Who's there?

Moo.

Moo who?

Make up your mind! Are you a cow or an owl?

35

Knock, knock.

Who's there?

Giraffe.

Giraffe who?

Giraffe anything to eat? I'm hungry!

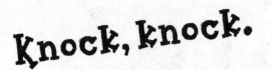

Knock, knock.

Who's there?

T. rex.

T. rex who?

There's a **T. rex** at your door and you want to know its name?

- - - - - - - - - - - - - - - - - - -

Knock, knock.

Who's there?

Two knee.

Two knee who?

Two-knee fish!

Knock, knock.

Who's there?

Sparrow.

Sparrow who?

Sparrow me the details and let me in.

---

Knock, knock.

Who's there?

Halibut.

Halibut who?

Halibut we go to the movies tonight?

Knock,
knock.

Who's there?

Lion.

Lion who?

Lion bed,
sleepyhead.

Knock, knock.

Who's there?

Pig.

Pig who?

Pig up your toys.
Your room's a mess!

Knock, knock.

Who's there?

Moose.

Moose who?

Moose you be so nosy?

Knock, knock.

Who's there?

Cock-a-doodle.

Cock-a-doodle who?

Not cock-a-doodle who, silly, cock-a-doodle-DOO!

Knock, knock.

Who's there?

Weasel.

Weasel who?

Weasel cookies. Would you like to buy some?

---

Knock, knock.

Who's there?

Cheetah.

Cheetah who?

Cheetahs never win and winners never cheat.

Knock, knock.

Who's there?

Parrot.

Parrot who?

Parrot who?
Parrot who?
Parrot who?

(PRO TIP: Use a parrot voice when you read this one!)

43

Knock, knock.

Who's there?

Koala.

Koala who?

Koala me whatever you like.

Knock, knock.

Who's there?

Toad.

Toad who?

Toad-ally awesome, that's what you are!

Knock, knock.

Who's there?

Amos.

Amos who?

Amos-quito!

Knock, knock.

Who's there?

Rhino.

Rhino who?

Rhino every knock-knock joke there is!

Knock, knock.

Who's there?

Who.

Who who?

Is there an owl in here?

Knock, knock.

Who's there?

Althea.

Althea
who?

Althea later
alligator!

Knock,
knock.

Who's
there?

Beehive.

Beehive
who?

Beehive yourself.

Knock, knock.

Who's there?

Cook.

Cook who?

Hey! Who are you calling a cuckoo?

Knock, knock.

Who's there?

Toucan.

Toucan who?

Toucan play this game!

49

Knock, knock.

Who's there?

Honey bee.

Honey bee who?

Honey, bee a dear and grab my jar of pickles.

Knock, knock.

Who's there?

Viper.

Viper who?

Viper nose. It's dripping!

50

Knock, knock.

Who's there?

Goat.

Goat who?

Goat to bed!
It's late.

Knock, knock.

Who's there?

Bach.

Bach who?

Bach, bach.
I'm a chicken.

Knock, knock.

Who's there?

Roach.

Roach who?

I roach you a message.
Didn't you get it?

---

Knock, knock.

Who's there?

Dinosaur.

Dinosaur who?

Dinosaurs don't say
"who." They roar!

Knock, knock.

Who's there?

Alpaca.

Alpaca who?

Alpaca suitcase, and
we can hit the road!

Knock, knock.

Who's there?

Iguana.

Iguana who?

Iguana hold your hand.

# BACK-TO-SCHOOL SILLIES

Knock, knock.

Who's there?

Dizzy.

Dizzy who?

Dizzy new teacher nice?

Knock, knock.

Who's there?

Abe.

Abe who?

Abe-C-D-E-F-G!

---

Knock, knock.

Who's there?

Gecko.

Gecko who?

Gecko-ing or you'll be late for school!

# Knock, knock.

Who's there?

Heidi.

Heidi who?

Heidi toy before the teacher sees!

Knock, knock.

Who's
there?

Ahmed.

Ahmed who?

Ahmed a mistake.
Give me an eraser!

Knock, knock.

Who's there?

Fonda.

Fonda who?

Fonda my new classmates.

Knock, knock.

Who's there?

Harv.

Harv who?

Harv you ready for the new school year?

Knock, knock.

Who's there?

Gluck.

Gluck who?

Gluck on the quiz!

Knock, knock.

Who's there?

Pencil.

Pencil who?

Pencil fall down if you don't wear a belt!

Knock, knock.

Who's there?

Rita.

Rita who?

Rita book. You might learn something!

Knock, knock.

Who's there?

Warner.

Warner who?

Warner sit next to me on the bus?

Knock, knock.

Who's there?

Betsy.

Betsy who?

Betsy of all, school starts again soon!

- - - - - - - - - - - - - - - - - - - - - - -

Knock, knock.

Who's there?

Sty.

Sty who?

Sty home from school if you feel sick!

Knock, knock.

Who's there?

Drew.

Drew who?

Drew a picture of my big toe in art class!

Knock, knock.

Who's there?

Jess.

Jess who?

Jess wait till I tell you about my new teachers!

Knock, knock.

Who's there?

Broken pencil.

Broken pencil who?

Forget it, there's no point!

Knock, knock.

Who's there?

Tennis.

Tennis who?

Tennis five
plus five.

Knock, knock.

Who's there?

Double.

Double who?

W!

Knock, knock.

Who's there?

B-4.

B-4 who?

B-4 you go to bed, you need to finish your homework!

Knock, knock.

Who's there?

Earl.

Earl who?

Earl be glad when school starts again!

Knock, knock.

Who's there?

Spell.

Spell who?

Okay, since you asked: W-H-O.

Knock, knock.

Who's there?

Teddy.

Teddy who?

Teddy is the first day of school!

Knock, knock.

Who's there?

Buzz.

Buzz
who?

Buzz will be here
soon, so hurry up!

# FOOD FUNNIES

**Knock, knock.**

**Who's there?**

**Omelet.**

**Omelet who?**

**Omelet smarter than you think!**

Knock, knock.

Who's there?

orange.

Orange who?

orange you going to answer the door?

Knock, knock.

Who's there?

Pasta.

Pasta who?

Pasta salt and pepper, please!

- - - - - - - - - - - - - - - - - - - - - - -

Knock, knock.

Who's there?

Fajita.

Fajita who?

Fajita another, I'll be stuffed!

Knock, knock.

Who's there?

Berry.

Berry who?

Berry nice to meet you!

Knock, knock.

Who's there?

Muffin.

Muffin who?

There's muffin the matter with me! How about you?

Knock, knock.

Who's there?

Pizza.

Pizza who?

Pizza really
nice guy!

Knock, knock.

Who's there?

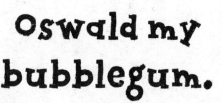

Oswald.

Oswald who?

Oswald my bubblegum.

Knock, knock.

Who's there?

Stew.

Stew who?

Stew early for bed!

- - - - - - - - - - - - - - - - - - - - - - - - -

Knock, knock.

Who's there?

Dairy.

Dairy who?

Dairy goes! Let's catch him!

77

Knock, knock.

Who's there?

Amile.

Amile who?

Amile fit for a king!

---

Knock, knock.

Who's there?

Chicken.

Chicken who?

Better chicken the oven—something's burning.

Knock, knock.

Who's there?

Turnip.

Turnip who?

Turnip the volume, I love this song!

Knock, knock.

Who's there?

Cereal.

Cereal who?

Cereal
pleasure to
meet you!

Knock, knock.

Who's there?

Pecan.

Pecan who?

Pecan someone your own size!

---

Knock, knock.

Who's there?

Quiche.

Quiche who?

Can I have a hug and a quiche?

Knock, knock.

Who's there?

Pudding.

Pudding who?

Pudding on shoes, then we can leave!

---

Knock, knock.

Who's there?

Icing.

Icing who?

Icing loudly so everyone can hear me!

Knock, knock.

Who's there?

Olive.

Olive who?

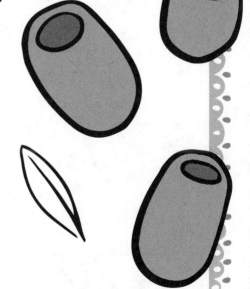

Olive right
next door
to you.

Knock, knock.
Who's there?
Banana.
Banana who?
Knock, knock.
Who's there?
Banana.
Banana who?
Knock, knock.
Who's there?
Orange.
Orange who?
Orange you glad I didn't say banana?

Knock, knock.

Who's there?

Beets.

Beets who?

Beets me!

Knock, knock.

Who's there?

Lettuce.

Lettuce who?

Lettuce in, it's cold out here.

85

Knock, knock.

Who's there?

Ketchup.

Ketchup who?

Ketchup with me and I'll tell you!

- - - - - - - - - - - - - - - - - - - - - - -

Knock, knock.

Who's there?

Annie.

Annie who?

Annie time I cut onions I cry!

Knock, knock.

Who's there?

Ice cream.

Ice cream
who?

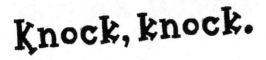

Ice cream
if you don't
let me in!

Knock, knock.

Who's there?

Donut.

Donut who?

Donut ask. It's top secret!

Knock, knock.

Who's there?

Broccoli.

Broccoli who?

Broccoli doesn't have a last name, silly!

- - - - - - - - - - - - - - - - - - - - -

Knock, knock.

Who's there?

Mango.

Mango who?

Man, go answer the door already!

Knock, knock.

Who's there?

West.

West who?

Let me know if you need a west from all these knock-knock jokes!

# Knock, knock.

## Who's there?

## Interrupting pirate.

## Interrup-

## ARRRRRRRRRR!

(PRO TIP: Use your best pirate voice for this joke!)

Knock, knock.

Who's there?

Mustache.

Mustache
who?

I mustache you
a question, but
I'll shave it for
later.

Knock, knock.

Who's there?

Ears.

Ears who?

Ears another joke for you!

Knock, knock.

Who's there?

Avenue.

Avenue who?

Avenue knocked on this door before?

93

Knock, knock.

Who's there?

Europe.

Europe who?

No, *you're a poo!*

- - - - - - - - - - - - - - -

Knock, knock.

Who's there?

Says.

Says who?

Says me, that's who!

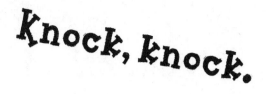

Knock, knock.

Who's there?

Comb.

Comb who?

Comb on in and sit a while!

Knock, knock.

Who's there?

Yukon.

Yukon, who?

Yukon say that again!

- - - - - - - - - - - - - - - - - - - - - - - - - -

Knock, knock.

Who's there?

Voodoo.

Voodoo, who?

Voodoo you think you are, asking all these questions?

Knock, knock.

Who's there?

Sofa.

Sofa who?

Sofa these have been some funny jokes!

- - - - - - - - - - - - - - - - - - - - -

Knock, knock.

Who's there?

Sweden.

Sweden who?

Sweden sour chicken!

Knock,
knock.

Who's there?

Hawaii.

Hawaii
who?

I'm fine.
Hawaii
you?

Knock, knock.

Who's there?

Lily pad.

Lily pad who?

Lily pad weather outside today. I hope it clears up!

Knock, knock.

Who's there?

Repeat.

Repeat who?

Who, who, who, who, who.

Knock, knock.

Who's there?

Ratio.

Ratio who?

Ratio to the end of the street!

Knock, knock.

Who's there?

I need a puh.

I need a puh who?

Then why don't you find a toilet?

------------------------------

Knock, knock.

Who's there?

Razor.

Razor who?

Razor hand and dance the boogie!

Knock, knock.

Who's there?

Bed.

Bed who?

Bed you can't guess who this is!

Knock, knock.

Who's there?

Leaf.

Leaf
who?

Leaf me
alone!

Knock, knock.

Who's there?

Itch.

Itch who?

Bless you!

- - - - - - - - - - - - - - - - - - -

Knock, knock.

Who's there?

Water.

Water who?

Water you doing in my house?

Knock, knock.

Who's there?

Tank.

Tank who?

You're welcome!

---

Knock, knock.

Who's there?

Armageddon.

Armageddon who?

Armageddon a little bored. Want to play?

Knock, knock.

Who's there?

Radio.

Radio who?

Radio not, here I come!

Knock, knock!

Who's there?

Ya.

Ya who?

Are you a cowboy?

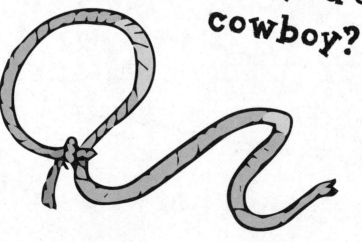

Knock, knock.

Who's there?

Dozen.

Dozen who?

Dozen anyone want to let me in?

---

Knock, knock.

Who's there?

Wooden shoe.

Wooden shoe who?

Wooden shoe like to hear another joke?

Knock, knock.

Who's there?

Haven.

Haven who?

Haven't you heard this one before?

---

Knock, knock.

Who's there?

Cargo.

Cargo who?

Cargo beep, beep!

# Knock, knock.

## Who's there?

## Cactus.

## Cactus who?

## Cactus makes perfect!

Knock, knock.

Who's there?

Stopwatch.

Stopwatch
who?

Stopwatch you're
doing and pay
attention!

Knock, knock.

Who's there?

Fiddle.

Fiddle who?

Fiddle make you happy, I'll tell you!

- - - - - - - - - - - - - - - - - - - - - - -

Knock, knock.

Who's there?

Thermos.

Thermos who?

Thermos be a better way to get your attention.

Knock, knock.

Who's there?

Venice.

Venice who?

Venice your mom getting home?

---

Knock, knock.

Who's there?

Ice.

Ice who?

Ice-y what you did there!

Knock, knock.

Who's there?

Nose.

Nose who?

I nose plenty more
knock-knock jokes!

Knock, knock.

Who's there?

Window.

Window who?

Window I get to tell you another joke?

Knock, knock.

Who's there?

Iran.

Iran who?

Iran all the way here to see you!

- - - - - - - - - - - - - - - - - - - - - -

Knock, knock.

Who's there?

Wire.

Wire who?

Wire you always asking "who's there?"

Knock, knock.

Who's there?

Atlas.

Atlas who?

Atlas, it's Valentine's Day!

Knock, knock.

Who's there?

Whale.

Whale who?

Whale you be
my valentine?

Knock, knock.

Who's there?

Al.

Al who?

Al be your
Valentine
if you'll
be mine.

BE MINE

120

Knock, knock.

Who's there?

Jamaica.

Jamaica who?

Jamaica Valentine for me yet?

- - - - - - - - - - - - - - - - - - - - - - - - - - -

Knock, knock.

Who's there?

Irish.

Irish who?

Irish you a happy St. Patrick's Day!

Knock, knock.

Who's there?

Clover.

Clover who?

Clover here and I'll tell you.

- - - - - - - - - - - - - - - - - - - -

Knock, knock.

Who's there?

Erin.

Erin who?

Erin as fast as I could but couldn't catch the leprechaun.

Knock, knock.

Who's there?

Potty.

Potty who?

Potty gold at the end of the rainbow.

Knock, knock.

Who's there?

Warren.

Warren who?

Warren anything green for St. Patrick's Day?

Knock, knock.

Who's there?

Alma.

Alma who?

Alma Easter candy is gone already!

- - - - - - - - - - - - - - - - - - - -

Knock, knock.

Who's there?

Howard.

Howard who?

Howard you like a chocolate bunny?

Hi!

125

Knock, knock.

Who's there?

Hoppy.

Hoppy who?

Hoppy Easter, everyone!

- - - - - - - - - - - - - - -

Knock, knock.

Who's there?

Carrie.

Carrie who?

Carrie my Easter basket, please. It's too heavy.

126

Knock, knock.

Who's there?

Arthur.

Arthur who?

Arthur more eggs we can decorate?

Knock, knock.

Who's there?

Philip.

Philip who?

Philip my bag with
Halloween candy,
please!

Knock, knock.

Who's there?

Witches.

Witches who?

Witches the way to
the haunted house?

Knock, knock.

Who's there?

Bee.

Bee who?

Bee-ware, all the ghosts are out on Halloween!

Knock, knock.

Who's there?

Gladys.

Gladys who?

Gladys Thanksgiving!

Knock, knock.

Who's there?

Dewey.

Dewey who?

Dewey have
to wait much
longer for the
turkey?

Knock, knock.

Who's there?

Tamara.

Tamara who?

Tamara we'll have a ton of leftovers!

---

Knock, knock.

Who's there?

Honey.

Honey who?

Honey-kkah is my favorite holiday!

Knock, knock.

Who's there?

Ho-ho.

Ho-ho who?

You know, your Santa impression could use a little work.

Knock, knock.

Who's there?

Olive.

Olive who?

Olive the other reindeer used to laugh at Rudolph!

Knock, knock.

Who's there?

Anna.

Anna who?

Anna partridge in a pear tree!

- - - - - - - - - - - - - - - - - -

Knock, knock.

Who's there?

Imma.

Imma who?

Imma dreaming of a white Christmas!

Knock, knock.

Who's there?

Mary.

Mary who?

Mary Christmas and Happy New Year!

---

Knock, knock.

Who's there?

Howie.

Howie who?

Howie going to stay up till midnight for the New Year? I'm tired!

Knock, knock.

Who's there?

Hannah.

Hannah who?

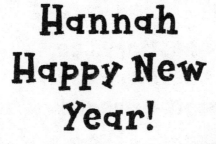

Hannah
Happy New
Year!

Sing the punchlines of these jokes!

Knock, knock.

Who's there?

Mary Lee.

Mary Lee who?

Mary Lee, Mary Lee, Mary Lee, Mary Lee, life is but a dream!

Knock, knock.

Who's there?

Barbara.

Barbara who?

Barbara
black
sheep,
have you
any wool?

Knock, knock.

Who's there?

Meow.

Meow
who?

Take me-ow to
the ball game!

Knock, knock.

Who's there?

Shelby.

Shelby who?

Shelby comin' 'round the mountain when she comes!

Knock, knock.

Who's there?

Ringo.

Ringo who?

Ringo 'round the rosie, a pocket full of posies!

Knock, knock.

Who's there?

Jacken.

Jacken who?

Jacken Jill went up the hill to fetch a pail of water!

---

Knock, knock.

Who's there?

Sombrero.

Sombrero who?

Sombrero-ver the rainbow!

Knock, knock.

Who's there?

Rocket.

Rocket who?

Rocket-bye baby, on the tree top!

Knock, knock.

Who's there?

Cheese.

Cheese, who?

For cheese a jolly good fellow!

Knock, knock.

Who's there?

Heigh.

Heigh who?

Heigh-ho, heigh-ho,
it's off to work we go!

---

Knock, knock.

Who's there?

Wendy.

Wendy who?

Wendy wind blows, the
cradle will fall!

Knock, knock.

Who's there?

Poppa.

Poppa who?

Poppa goes the weasel!

- - - - - - - - - - - - - - - - - - - - - - - -

Knock, knock.

Who's there?

Twin.

Twin who?

Twin-kle, twinkle, little star.

Knock,
knock.

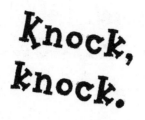

Who's
there?

Izzy.

Izzy who?

Izzy bitsy spider
went up the
water spout!

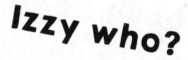

Knock, knock.

Who's there?

Rhoda.

Rhoda who?

Row, row,
Rhoda boat,
gently down
the stream!

Knock, knock.

Who's there?

Free.

Free who?

Free blind mice. See how they run!

- - - - - - - - - - - - - - - - - - - - - - -

Knock, knock.

Who's there?

Joel.

Joel who?

Joel Macdonald had a farm, E-I-E-I-O!

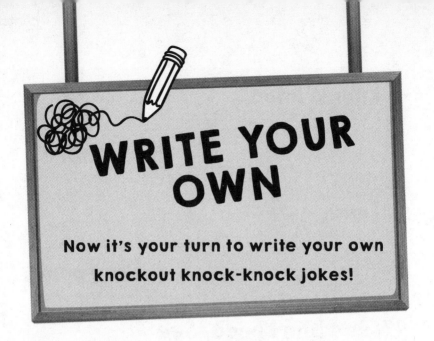

# WRITE YOUR OWN

Now it's your turn to write your own knockout knock-knock jokes!

PRO TIP: Start with the classic lines "Knock, knock" and "Who's there?", and then add a name or word that will create a funny pun and punchline at the end! Try it below!

Knock, knock.

Who's there?

_____

_____ who?

_____
_____

**Check out these other knee-slapper books from embarrassing dad and jokester Jimmy Niro!**

SILLY LAUGHS FOR THE WHOLE FAMILY

THE **ULTIMATE GROSS CHALLENGE**

JIMMY NIRO

A BATTLE OF YUCKY CHOICES

Who can LAUGH LAST?

THE **ULTIMATE JOKE CHALLENGE**

Battle the whole family with these SILLY JOKES!

JIMMY NIRO

350+ SILLY, LAUGH-OUT-LOUD JOKES
FOR THE WHOLE FAMILY!

# DAD
## JOKES
## FOR
## KIDS!

THEY'RE
DINO-MITE!

JIMMY NIRO

# DAD
# JOKES

the GOOD.
the BAD.
the TERRIBLE.

Jimmy Niro

JIMMY NIRO

# DAD
## JOKES

HOLIDAY
EDITION!

YULE LOVE THEM!

SUPER!!!

# DAD
## JOKES

SAVING THE WORLD,
ONE BAD JOKE
AT A TIME

JIMMY NIRO